Indians of the Great Lakes

An Illustrated History For Children

John Mitchell and Tom Woodruff

for Patrick, Kelsey, Dudley, Mary, Matt, and Drew

Suttons Bay Publications
301 St. Joseph, Box 361
Suttons Bay, Michigan 49682

Not long ago, lumberjacks cut down the last old forests of the Great Lakes region. Trees that stood for centuries were soon replaced by the farms and towns, roads and cars, and cities and suburbs of our modern world. Today, our way of life continues to tame nature and shape it to our needs. Our houses shut out cold, cars carry us to stores where we buy food and clothes. The natural world around us is often forgotten as we hurry from door to door.

For thousands of years, tall trees grew close to the shores of all five Great Lakes and covered the region in a dark, green forest. During this time, a series of different Indian nations settled the beautiful land and called the forests their home. Though the language and customs of the early people changed, all Great Lakes natives lived in close contact with the lakes and woods around them. They understood the demands of each of the four seasons and planned their lives around the changes that nature brought. Like the sun and the moon and the rain, the ancient trees shading their villages were part of their everyday world.

Each of the five Great Lakes is huge, together they stretch for thousands of miles across the heart of North America. Long before roads and cars cut across the country, the people of the Great Lakes lived where woods and water met, and the environment shaped their lives. People slept and dressed and traveled in products they made by hand. By the light of the campfire, one generation taught the next the secrets of how to survive in the forest. Some native people led hard lives, others enjoyed peace and plenty. The success or failure of all Native Americans was closely linked to the natural world.

Five hundred years ago, Europeans crossed the Atlantic Ocean in sailing ships and found a land and people new to them. Europeans called the people they met Indians, for they believed they had landed near the Asian country of India. In fact, they had come to North America, a continent long enjoyed by people with a history and laws of their own. Today the word Indian includes all Native Americans whose ten-thousand-year history is an important part of our American heritage.

The Earth is a very old place that has changed on its surface many times. When the planet was young, fiery volcanoes shook the land and hot gases poisoned the air. There was no life, anywhere. Millions of years passed and heavy rains poured down, covering much of the earth in warm, shallow seas. Soon many strange and beautiful plants and animals filled these seas and later moved on to land. The forms of life changed often to survive the changing environment on Earth.

Some early life forms left their imprint in rocks called fossils. Fossils of leaves and bones show us many pictures of our ancient planet. Once this was a warmer world, where huge dinosaurs roamed through steamy swamps long before people walked the Earth.

Slowly the Earth cooled and thick sheets of ice called glaciers covered much of the land. Dinosaurs and many other forms of life died out and became extinct. Only a few areas in Asia and Africa remained warm. The first people on Earth lived in these warm places.

The period before people kept written record of their lives is known as prehistoric time. Scientists piece together the lives of prehistoric people from bits of evidence they left scattered about their ancient camps. Bones found near campfires tell us what people ate. Buried tools help explain the type of work early people performed.

The first people on Earth were hunters who roamed in small bands in search of food. They learned how to make fires, use simple tools, and build shelters against the weather. They drew pictures of their lives on rock walls and passed their history down from storyteller to storyteller. In time, people began to travel wherever they could find enough food to keep them alive.

The Earth remained cool for thousands of years. Every year, more snow fell in winter than would melt during the summer. In many places the glaciers grew to more than a mile thick. Much of the Earth's water was held frozen in the giant glaciers, causing the level of the oceans to fall. This period is known as the Ice Age.

The low water level of the oceans during the time of the glaciers exposed areas of dry land that are now covered with water. While today Asia and North America are separated by the Bering Sea, in times past a wide bridge of dry land linked the two places. During the Ice Age, part of the Bering Sea dried up and a continent called Beringia connected Asia to North America.

Asia

Beringia

North America

Bering Sea

People hunted the many animals that fed on the grassy meadows between glaciers. In time, they followed the herds of animals through Asia, across Beringia, and into North America. The new continent proved friendly to life, and roving bands of hunters scattered throughout the land.

Tall fields of grass grew from the rich soils of North America. The grasses fed the many fur covered animals of the Ice Age. Prehistoric Great Lakes hunters charged mastodons, musk ox, and other huge animals and killed them with stone tipped spears. Nothing was wasted, for the natives used every piece of the kill for food, clothing, or shelter.

One giant mastodon could feed a family of roving hunters for weeks. The tough, wooly mastodon skin was cut into clothes and blankets to keep out the cold. Extra meat was dried in the sun or smoked by the fire and saved for harder times. Every year, skills and weapons improved. Family groups grew larger as the hunters' catch provided the food and clothing needed to survive.

12,000 Years ago

10,000 Years ago

4,000 Years ago

Ten thousand years ago, the earth began to warm and the glaciers melted back to the north. The water from melting glaciers filled low spots in the center of North America and the Great Lakes began to form. The glaciers continued to melt, constantly changing the shape, size, and depth of the Great Lakes. In time, the water filled then overflowed the limits of each lake and drained east to the Atlantic Ocean. The water in all the oceans rose, again cutting North America off from the rest of the world.

A warmer climate brought other changes to the environment of the Great Lakes. Giant pine and hardwood trees rose from the grasslands, covering the earth in dark forests. Mastodons and other large animals that depended on the grasslands for food died out and became extinct. The forests grew and thickened and a new group of plants and animals made the Great Lakes region their home.

Small bands of people ventured into the dark forests of the Great Lakes and fished and camped near freshwater streams. In this land of four seasons, the Indians were nomadic, moving with the changing weather to the best hunting, fishing, and gathering sites. The Indians developed bows and arrows for hunting and gathered wild berries, roots, and nuts to add to their meals. They learned to sew together the skins of animals for clothing and stretch it across wooden poles to build their homes.

The forests of the Great Lakes grew thick and dark like jungles. There were no roads and the Indians settled near water, using lakes and rivers as natural highways. The religions of the native people honored the great spirits who created the beautiful forests around them. The people lived in harmony with nature and believed that every creature, large and small, was an important part of their world.

Scattered groups of Indian families grew in number and began to unite in larger groups called tribes. Over time, many different tribes formed within the Great Lakes region, each with their own unique way of living. One of the first great tribes of the Great Lakes region is today known as the Old Copper Indians.

Five thousand years ago, melting glaciers continued to shape the shores of Lake Superior. This cold, rocky country was then home to the Old Copper Indians. The Indians gathered copper along the shores of Lake Superior during the summer and hammered the soft metal into tools and jewelry, fish hooks and spear points, and other useful objects. When the weather cooled, the Old Copper Indians traveled along the edge of the lakes in canoes filled with copper products. They traded in peace with the people they met along the way. Their copper artwork has been found in ancient campsites and graves from the Atlantic Ocean to the Rocky Mountains.

Like many cultures that would follow them in prehistoric times, the Old Copper Indians disappeared long ago, leaving behind only copper tools and abandoned mines as proof they ever existed. What happened to the Old Copper Indians is still a mystery today.

The first Indians of the Great Lakes were nomadic, moving from campsite to campsite in the continual search for food. They needed to hunt and gather from large areas in order to stay alive. They traveled long distances as the seasons and the weather changed the best place to live.

Over three thousand years ago, Great Lakes natives began to grow crops rather than depend on wild food sources alone. Their campsites included small gardens of beans, sunflowers, and squash. Skilled Indian farmers experimented with plants and were the first to grow corn and potatoes, and harvest wild rice. In time, corn became the most important food crop for the Indians.

Farming freed the Indians from a life of constant travel. They became less dependent on the cycle of the seasons and could settle in one area without fear of starvation. After they learned to grow their own food, the number of people living in the Great Lakes region grew steadily.

For the next two thousand years, Indians known as Mound Builders settled the rich river valleys of the Great Lakes region. Though they lived at different times, the Adena, Hopewell, and Mississippian people shared the custom of building large, mysterious mounds of earth as gathering centers, graves, and places of worship.

The Adena Indians were the first of the Mound Builders. They lived in a time of natural plenty when hunting, gathering, and growing crops easily provided for the needs of their people. The Adena had the time to decorate pottery and carve fine figures in stone. Hundreds worked together carrying baskets of dirt to build mounds shaped like snakes, birds, and other animals.

The Hopewell were the second mound building Indians of the Great Lakes region. Burial ceremonies around their mounds were sacred events that united the widespread nation. The Hopewell were a religious people who believed in life after death. Beautiful jewelry and art objects decorate the skeletons that lay in ancient Hopewell mounds.

Rather than make weapons and fight wars, the Hopewell planted fields of corn and traded with their neighbors. Everyone benefited. Agriculture and trade brought peace and prosperity to the Hopewell people.

The Mississippians were the last and largest group of Mound Builders. The Mississippians were serious farmers, growing enough food to support the biggest settlement ever built by Indians of the Great Lakes. By the year 1200, their main town of Cahokia was home to over forty thousand people. Cahokia's central mound, where powerful priests led religious ceremonies, was bigger at its base than the Great Pyramid of Egypt.

The different Mound Builders brought peace to the Great Lakes region. Mound building united scattered families into one people with a common goal. Their long trade routes crossed borders and mixed together the products and ideas of different people. When the last of the mound building nations fell apart, many tribes along the Lakes lost contact with each other. Traders learned the ways of warriors as fights between rival Indian tribes increased.

Cahokia

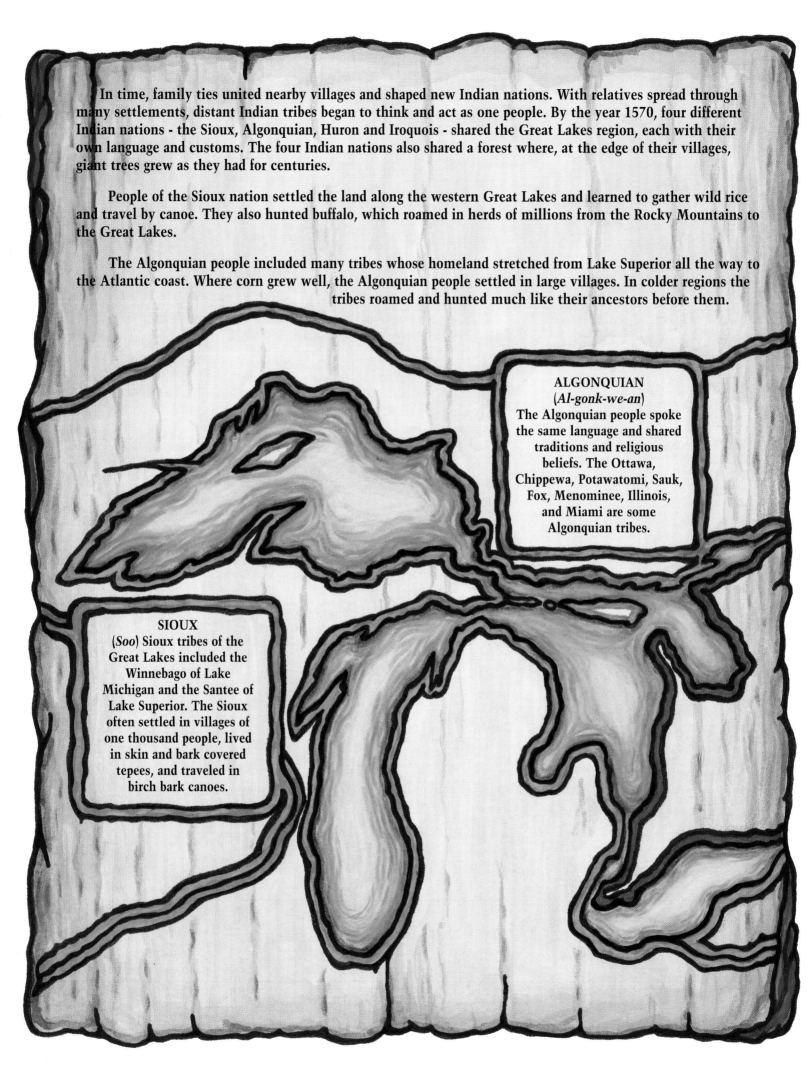

In time, family ties united nearby villages and shaped new Indian nations. With relatives spread through many settlements, distant Indian tribes began to think and act as one people. By the year 1570, four different Indian nations - the Sioux, Algonquian, Huron and Iroquois - shared the Great Lakes region, each with their own language and customs. The four Indian nations also shared a forest where, at the edge of their villages, giant trees grew as they had for centuries.

People of the Sioux nation settled the land along the western Great Lakes and learned to gather wild rice and travel by canoe. They also hunted buffalo, which roamed in herds of millions from the Rocky Mountains to the Great Lakes.

The Algonquian people included many tribes whose homeland stretched from Lake Superior all the way to the Atlantic coast. Where corn grew well, the Algonquian people settled in large villages. In colder regions the tribes roamed and hunted much like their ancestors before them.

ALGONQUIAN
(*Al-gonk-we-an*)
The Algonquian people spoke the same language and shared traditions and religious beliefs. The Ottawa, Chippewa, Potawatomi, Sauk, Fox, Menominee, Illinois, and Miami are some Algonquian tribes.

SIOUX
(*Soo*) Sioux tribes of the Great Lakes included the Winnebago of Lake Michigan and the Santee of Lake Superior. The Sioux often settled in villages of one thousand people, lived in skin and bark covered tepees, and traveled in birch bark canoes.

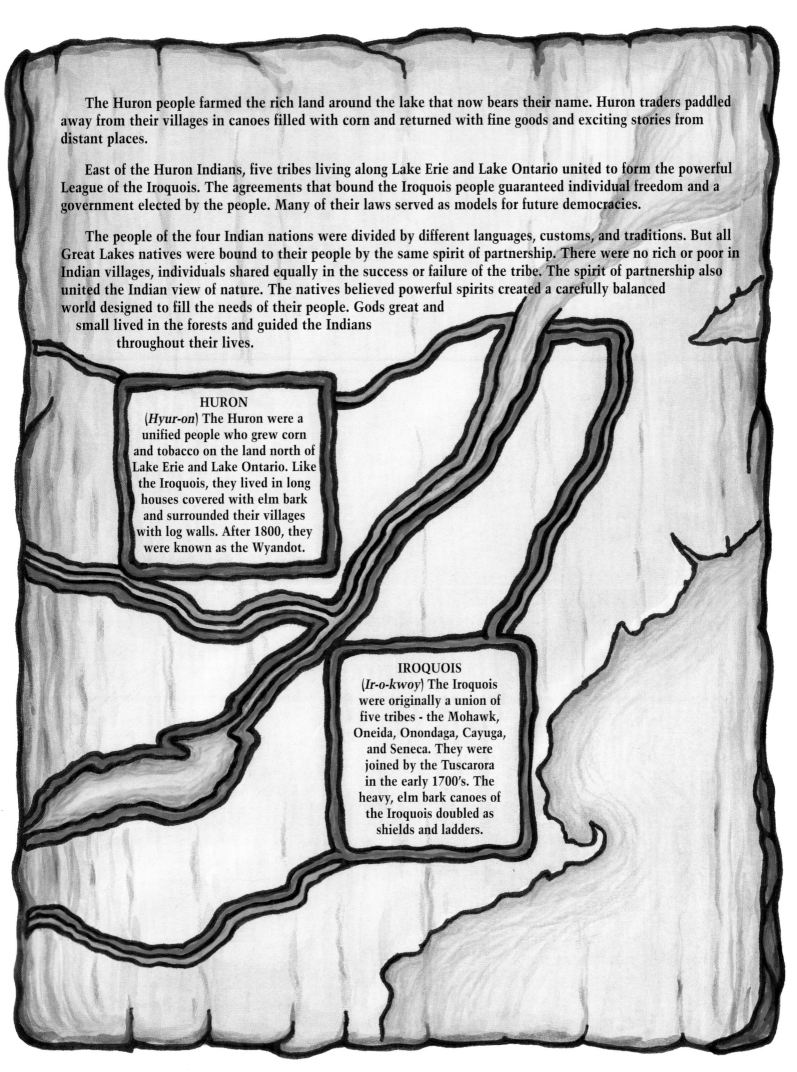

The Huron people farmed the rich land around the lake that now bears their name. Huron traders paddled away from their villages in canoes filled with corn and returned with fine goods and exciting stories from distant places.

East of the Huron Indians, five tribes living along Lake Erie and Lake Ontario united to form the powerful League of the Iroquois. The agreements that bound the Iroquois people guaranteed individual freedom and a government elected by the people. Many of their laws served as models for future democracies.

The people of the four Indian nations were divided by different languages, customs, and traditions. But all Great Lakes natives were bound to their people by the same spirit of partnership. There were no rich or poor in Indian villages, individuals shared equally in the success or failure of the tribe. The spirit of partnership also united the Indian view of nature. The natives believed powerful spirits created a carefully balanced world designed to fill the needs of their people. Gods great and small lived in the forests and guided the Indians throughout their lives.

HURON
(*Hyur-on*) The Huron were a unified people who grew corn and tobacco on the land north of Lake Erie and Lake Ontario. Like the Iroquois, they lived in long houses covered with elm bark and surrounded their villages with log walls. After 1800, they were known as the Wyandot.

IROQUOIS
(*Ir-o-kwoy*) The Iroquois were originally a union of five tribes - the Mohawk, Oneida, Onondaga, Cayuga, and Seneca. They were joined by the Tuscarora in the early 1700's. The heavy, elm bark canoes of the Iroquois doubled as shields and ladders.

For hundreds of years, rival Iroquois tribes battled each other along the shores of the eastern Great Lakes. Sick of fighting and dying, five tribes united in the year 1570 to form the powerful League of the Iroquois. League laws linked the five tribes together as states in a Great Lakes nation. The Iroquois people chose the pine tree as their symbol, with each member tribe adding strength to the tree.

Inside the tall log walls surrounding Iroquois villages, families crowded together in curved top homes called long houses. Often dozens of people from several generations lived under the same roof. As heads of the long houses, women played an important role in Iroquois society. Women selected the leaders who spoke for the tribes at yearly League of the Iroquois councils. When an Iroquois couple married, it was the man who changed his family name.

Outside the safety of village walls, Iroquois women raised fields of corn, a plant worshipped by the nation as a giver of life. The Iroquois were skilled farmers and depended on their crops for most of their meals. Dried corn fed villages of several thousand people through the long winters. Iroquois feasts celebrated the planting, raising, and harvesting of corn.

The Iroquois believed that many spirits, both good and evil, dwelled in the lakes and woods of their homeland. The bodies and souls of the Iroquois were part of the natural world controlled by these powerful spiritual forces.

Members of the False Face Society carved masks to match the faces of spirits they saw in dreams and visions. Masks were carved from living trees to capture their healing power. When the Indians wore the masks, they took on the strength of the trees and the spirits. The Iroquois used the magic of the masks to heal the sick, bless their crops, and give courage to their warriors.

Iroquois hunters doubled as warriors in raids outside their homeland. Individual courage and daring in battle brought honor to an entire family. In time, the Iroquois enjoyed few friends outside their League. Their warlike traditions often made enemies of their neighbors. Few dared to challenge an Iroquois tribe, for all five tribes fought together if any one were attacked.

The Huron Indians settled the fertile land shaped by the waters of Lake Huron, Lake Erie, and Lake Ontario. They called themselves Wendat, the people of the peninsula. Skilled Huron farmers worked the rich soil of their homeland and often grew more corn and tobacco than their people could use.

Dark old forests began where the Huron cornfields ended. Near Lake Erie and Lake Ontario, where their borders met, Iroquois raiders made the forest a dangerous place for Huron hunters and traders. While they had once been a common people, and shared a language and the long house way of life, the Huron and Iroquois nations were now bitter enemies.

Huron hunters wore body armor when they traveled the ancient forests. Several times each year hunters formed long lines through the woods, and by making noise and marching, they chased wild animals forward into wooden pens. All members of the tribe shared the catch. Bears were captured live and kept as pets or fattened up for special feasts. Deer were killed for food and their skin was made into clothing, moccasins, rope, and other useful items.

North of Iroquois raiding parties, the Huron people traveled freely in birch bark canoes. Hurons in canoes used lakes and rivers like roads to speed through the thick forests of their homeland. They traded corn and tobacco in lands far beyond their borders. When the fishing was good, they hauled trout from rapids and river mouths and netted whitefish along the many islands of Lake Huron.

Every ten years the Huron Nation celebrated the Feast of the Dead. The festival began when families from all over the Huron peninsula met in a central village. They carried with them the bones of relatives who had died since the last feast. The bones were cleaned, wrapped in furs, then buried together. The Huron believed the ceremony freed the souls of the dead and allowed them to join their ancestors. The festival also brought together the living and strengthened the bond between all Huron people.

The Algonquian people included dozens of independent tribes spread all across the Great Lakes region. The scattered Algonquian tribes shared a language and religion and often traded with each other. But there was no one leader or center of government for all the people. Chiefs led as many villages as chose to follow their advice.

Where it was too cold to grow corn, Algonquian tribes lived on the move, as their ancestors had for centuries. They camped near water and traveled by canoe when seasons changed the best place to find food. Small villages of several hundred people could quickly pack up their light, bark covered shelters and be ready to go. Home was often a place where the day's fishing, hunting, and gathering ended.

The roaming tribes were peaceful people content to live on the riches nature had to offer. Although they had no central government, religious ceremonies often brought the various tribes together in peace. Leaders called shamans traveled between villages and explained the meaning of dreams and visions. The Indians believed powerful spirits lived among all of nature, bringing sickness or health, hunger or plenty.

Good soil and steady rains made the land between Lake Michigan and Lake Huron an ideal place to grow crops. Here Algonquian tribes settled in large villages of dome-shaped wigwams, growing corn, squash and beans. The Algonquian people loved to hunt and fish. Hunters were often away from their villages, searching the woods for game.

One of the best hunts followed the first storms of winter, when deep snow slowed the speed of moose, elk, and other large animals. Algonquian hunters strapped on hand-made snowshoes and chased the animals until they became trapped in drifts. Well-aimed arrows brought a quick end to the struggle. The whole Algonquian village celebrated a successful hunt, for it guaranteed weeks of food during the cold winter.

Trade linked the independent Algonquian tribes and helped them share the wealth of the Great Lakes. If the crops of one tribe failed, neighbors would bring them food. Caring for each other was at the heart of Algonquian society - every individual was an important member of the tribe. Leaders were often the last in line to share the wealth of the hunt. Customs and traditions also served as laws uniting the widespread people.

White birch trees grew tall throughout the Great Lakes forests. Indians learned to fashion the skin of the birch tree - tough, waterproof, birch bark - into many items they used everyday. Birch bark proved to be an ideal material for people on the move. The bark added little weight to a basket of corn or a water pouch, and large pieces rolled up like paper. Birch bark buckets caught the sap from maple trees which was boiled down to make syrup. A bed of birch bark under fur blankets kept the dampness away. If something made of birch bark broke far away from home, repair parts could be cut from the nearest birch tree.

Skilled Indian workers knew the secrets of birch bark. During winter, birch bark grew thick and strong like rubber. Using sharpened shells for knives, Indians cut the thick bark from the tree trunks in spring and set it aside for making canoes. The thinner, lighter summer bark covered baskets and kept wind and rain out of their homes.

Before Europeans came to the Indian homelands, there were no horses in America. On land, Great Lakes Indians carried everything by hand. Foot paths through the forest were filled with mosquitoes, darkness, and the danger of enemy attack.

The Indians of the Great Lakes created birch bark canoes to solve their travel problems. Rather than chop down trees and build roads, natives paddled birch bark canoes on the lakes and rivers that ran through their forests. The bark canoes were fast and light and easy to carry and turned the waters of the Great Lakes into highways for the Indians.

Whole villages worked together building birch bark canoes. First, wooden stakes were driven into the ground to hold loose sheets of bark in place. Then a light wooden frame was built inside the bark to give the canoe its shape and strength. Skilled men and women used tree roots to lace a skin of birch bark tightly to the wooden skeleton. Children helped seal the bark seams with sticky pine pitch. During the warm seasons, the strong and beautiful canoes were used everyday by Huron, Algonquian, and Sioux travelers.

Treeless plains of grass stretched from the Rocky Mountains to the forests of the Great Lakes. For centuries, herds of buffalo fed on the grasses and fattened into huge animals. The Sioux settled the lands west of Lake Superior and Lake Michigan where the forest of the Great Lakes met the plains. They often hunted buffalo, and deer and wild rice were also important foods for the Sioux tribes.

Before they had horses, the Sioux used surprise to hunt the strong and dangerous buffalo. To start the hunt, the Sioux dressed in the fur of wolves to trick the buffalo. Hunters crawled slowly through the tall grass until they came close to the herd. By instinct, buffalo did not run from wolves but turned in groups to face their attack. Indian spears and arrows struck the buffalo before they could turn and run.

Nothing from the buffalo was wasted. First the Sioux feasted on fresh meat, then leftovers were smoked and dried for future meals. Buffalo skin was used for tepees and clothes. Sioux hunters had little effect on the size of the great herds. For every big buffalo killed, several more young buffalo were born.

Campfires along the Great Lakes lit the many villages of the Indian nations. Nighttime ceremonies celebrated their union with nature and honored the spirits who influenced their world. With no written language, the circle of people around the campfire was a theater where Indian storytellers kept history and traditions alive.

When fires turned to coals, and children slept in their parents arms, elders spoke the stories of a strange, new people sighted at the edge of the forest. The newcomers carried sticks that killed by spitting fire, and some of the strangers' white faces were covered with hair. They wore odd clothes and talked with words never heard before in Indian country.

Few natives understood that the strangers would soon change the Indian way of life forever.

In the year 1492, Christopher Columbus sailed from Europe, a land separated from North America by the Atlantic Ocean. Before Columbus crossed the Atlantic and came upon the home of the Indians, the people living in the two faraway places knew nothing of each other.

The voyages of Columbus excited the people of Europe. They imagined a wide open country filled with many riches. Soon kings and queens and wealthy merchants built many sailing ships to cross the Atlantic Ocean. Explorers returned with stories of a land where ancient forests grew close to the water as far as the eye could see. The Europeans believed the new world waiting across the Atlantic Ocean was theirs for the taking.

On the shores of North America, the Indians greeted their Europeans guests with curiosity. Immediately the two different cultures began to mix. Indians tried on cloth coats and hats; Europeans paddled around in canoes. Neither people would ever be the same again.

The European sailing powers of France, England, and Spain raced each other to claim a part of North America. Just as different Indian nations struggled to control the Great Lakes, these three countries often fought each other in Europe. They carried their quarrels with them on their voyages to North America.

Spanish ships sailed south along Florida to the islands of the Caribbean and beyond. The English explored the middle Atlantic coast. The French traveled north to where the St. Lawrence River empties the waters of the Great Lakes into the Atlantic Ocean.

Although European powers claimed the shores of North America where their ships patrolled, on land they were at the mercy of the Indians. Most early European settlements would have failed without the help of the native people.

Europeans and Indians had been separated since the earliest days of people on earth. When they first met in North America, each people lived in ways different from the other. Europeans crowded the decks of wooden sailing ships, Indians paddled by in beautiful bark canoes. The Europeans wore cloth clothes, the Indians animal skins and furs. The visitors carried steel knives and hatchets, the natives cut with sharpened shells and stones. The Europeans recorded their stories in books, Indians passed them down around campfires.

The French were the first Europeans to reach the Great Lakes. Using the waters of the St. Lawrence River as a highway, the French traveled quickly inland. For the first five hundred miles, the St. Lawrence was wide and deep enough for big French sailing ships. Where the river narrowed and rapids began, explorers used Indian canoes to reach the Great Lakes.

Each new landing of the French in Indian country brought people from two faraway corners of the world together for the first time. The Indians living along the St. Lawrence welcomed the strangers. When they allowed the French to enter their territories, the written history of Europeans in the Great Lakes region began.

The Indians of the Great Lakes believed the land they lived on was borrowed from the earth. Individual Indians did not own land and national territory was shared among all members of the tribe. Whole villages moved regularly to new hunting and fishing sites and planted their corn in fresh soil. In Europe, kings and queens and a few wealthy families owned most of the land. They divided the countryside with fence posts to mark their private property. Indian land beside the St. Lawrence River was free of property markers. The newcomers thought the land was theirs for the taking and claimed it for the king of France.

The first Indians to visit France were surprised by what they saw. Outside the palaces of the rich, people lived in poverty. Great Lakes Indians shared their wealth, and all people were equal and important members of the tribe. The Indians were also troubled by the strict way the French treated their children. Children ran freely through Indian villages and the noise of their playing was a welcome sound.

The first French settlement, named Quebec, was built along the St. Lawrence River in 1608. Nearby Algonquian and Huron Indians made friends with the French and helped them survive the cold winter.

After the snow melted, French soldiers traveled with their Indian allies in a raid on the Iroquois nation. The battle began when the French opened fire with muskets, a weapon the Iroquois had never seen before. Several Iroquois chiefs were killed instantly, others turned and ran in terror. The Iroquois would never forgive or forget the French attack.

The League of the Iroquois brought together five tribes as states in one nation. The union was strong, for Iroquois law made life better for all five tribes. Following the French attack on the Mohawk tribe of the Iroquois, the four other Iroquois tribes - the Oneida, Onondaga, Cayuga and Seneca - voted to send their nation to war against the French.

The Iroquois attacked the French and their Indian allies in all directions. The loosely bound Algonquian tribes failed to unite against the Iroquois advance, and one by one they fell. The Huron nation lived in fear as Iroquois war parties began to invade their homeland. When rival tribes were conquered, Iroquois families adopted prisoners to replace warriors killed in battle. Every year, the Iroquois nation grew stronger and larger as it fanned out across the Great Lakes region.

The English settled the Atlantic coast from Maine to Georgia. As they traveled west into the dark forests, the English met the Iroquois, the enemy of their enemy the French. The English joined the Iroquois in their war of revenge against the French, giving them rifles, metal knives, hatchets, and other war supplies. Great Lakes Indians dropped their stone weapons and entered the forests with more deadly arms from Europe. By the year 1625, musket fire echoed from Iroquois villages along Lake Ontario to small Algonquian hunting camps around Lake Superior.

Indians of the Great Lakes were quick to find that many things made in Europe were superior to what they used. Sharp metal knives cut better than stones and shells. Cooking was easier in metal kettles than clay pots. Bows and arrows could not match the power of deadly rifles.

The Great Lakes forests were filled with fur-bearing animals, most importantly the beaver. Europeans had killed most of the fur-bearing animals on their continent, so coats and hats made of furs from the Great Lakes quickly became popular. Ships landing in Europe with a load of furs made their owners rich. Trading posts along the Atlantic coast prospered, and settlers poured in. Soon many Europeans traveled deep into the Great Lakes country to trade metal goods for Indian furs. Other Indian products became popular in Europe. Corn and potatoes were grown on European farms. Indian tobacco made smoking common place.

Each year, more and more Europeans paddled into the Great Lakes region for a chance to get rich trading for furs. They camped with their Indian hosts on the frontier and learned to enjoy the Indian way of life. Traders married into Indian families and were welcomed as one of the tribe. As the two people mixed, the Indians of the Great Lakes began to lose many of their traditional ways. The art of making pottery and fine stone tools, and skill with bows and arrows, no longer seemed important. Their partnership with nature was ending. Now Native Americans killed beaver to trade for knives, guns, blankets, and other things they needed.

Throughout North America, children from European families thought of their home as the land where they were born. They lived with Indian neighbors and learned about the native belief in individual freedom and the Indian custom of choosing their own leaders. Their parents' world of kings and queens seemed strange and far away.

Despite the increase in traders, the Great Lakes remained firmly in the hands of the powerful Indian nations. Europeans entered Indian territory only with their permission. The Iroquois tightened their grip on the southern Great Lakes, trapping furs from the region for trade with their English allies. The Algonquian and Huron people, together with the French, held the north country, where animals with the best furs lived.

By the year 1640, skilled Iroquois and Huron hunters had killed most of the beaver in the rivers of their homelands. The ancient Indian custom of living in balance with nature was abandoned. The Great Lakes wilderness became a more dangerous place as the two long-time enemies struggled to control the flow of furs from other tribes.

There were still many beaver north of the Great Lakes, the homeland of the Chippewa, Menominee, and other Algonquian tribes. In this cold country, hunters trapped beaver in the dead of winter, when their fur grew the thickest. When the river ice melted, they filled their canoes with furs and paddled to the nearest trading center.

Great Lakes furs had to be carried to the Atlantic coast and loaded on ships bound for Europe. First the furs had to pass through the territory of either the Huron or Iroquois. The European powers bought all the furs their Indian allies could supply, and the Great Lakes nations became further divided trying to meet the demand. All the while, sailing ships from Europe carried a steady stream of explorers and settlers to North America. Indians slowly lost their homelands along the Atlantic coast.

Every year, Europeans built forts deeper and deeper into Indian territory. In many places, Europeans began to outnumber the native people. Homeless Indians, forced from their lands along the Atlantic coast, wandered into the Great Lakes region and crossed tribal borders. Indians of the Great Lakes began to see they too could lose their ancient lands.

Great Lakes Indians loved their children and made decisions with the interests of their young in mind. Many tribal elders began to wonder, "What will be left for the future?" Some leaders urged their people to return to ancient ways. But nothing could stop the forces of change sweeping the Great Lakes country.

Outside the log walls of European forts, trade in furs held an uneasy peace together. While many Europeans shared the forests with Indians as friends, their leaders often acted as invaders. Promises made in treaties were often kept only as long as the Indian nations stayed strong.

As the Great Lakes Indian nations began to question the value of their friendship with European allies, a new enemy swept their villages, killing many more people than were lost in war. This enemy was a disease called smallpox.

Smallpox was common in Europe, and people there developed a resistance to the disease. In North America, the Indians' outdoor lifestyle and close contact with nature kept them in good health. At the time of their first contact, Indians lived longer than Europeans. But Indians had no defense against this horrible disease. Herbal medicines and spiritual healers failed to stop its spread. Whole families died without mercy. The powerful medicine societies that held Great Lakes nations together were helpless against the new invader.

The Huron nation suffered the most. The Huron had welcomed French traders and missionaries into their villages and with the French came smallpox. Within ten years, the Huron lost half their people to the disease. The Iroquois, while making peace with the British, had kept them out of their towns. They suffered less from smallpox. The Iroquois attacked the sick and weakened Huron, driving them from their homeland. What was left of the shattered Huron nation moved west, never to return.

The Iroquois then turned on the Chippewa, Ottawa, and Potawatomi tribes of Algonquian people whose forest-covered lands were home to many fur bearing animals. These tribes were united as the Three Fires, but together they could not stop the Iroquois warriors' advance. The Three Fires abandoned their homes in Michigan and moved west. In turn, the tribes of the western Great Lakes were pushed onto the plains.

Chaos and destruction followed deadly smallpox as hunger for furs ruled North America. By the year 1680, the Iroquois controlled most of the Great Lakes region.

The French saw the danger as their Indian allies lost ground across the Great Lakes region. They built a string of forts to increase their power and help their Algonquian and Huron friends regain their homeland. Supplied with French guns, many tribes of the Great Lakes united and rose against the Iroquois. By the year 1700, Indians allied with the French drove the invading Iroquois back to New York, the land of their ancestors.

The small French population in North America was content to trap and trade and leave the forests to the Indians. But along the Atlantic coast, the poor of England arrived by the shipload and rejoiced at the chance to own land. They cut down trees and planted crops and built houses and barns. Fights along the edge of the forest increased as English settlers pushed toward the Great Lakes.

In the year 1756, a war between the French and English in Europe spread to North America. The Great Lakes Indians, torn by disease and war and dependent on their allies for strength, split again. The Iroquois joined the English, the Algonquian and Huron people united with the French. The French and their Indian allies struck first, capturing English forts near Lake Ontario. But the English army was larger, and in the year 1759, the French capitol of Quebec fell. The French soon surrendered all of their forts along the Great Lakes, leaving their Indian allies to make the best peace they could.

When they first entered the Great Lakes forests, Europeans needed the help of Indians to survive. The newcomers brought many presents and peace offerings to win their trust. With France defeated, and English power on the rise, the gifts stopped. English leaders did not care if the Indians of the Great Lakes were their friends.

Angered by the way the English treated his people, the Algonquian leader Pontiac plotted to force them out of the Great Lakes region. In the year 1763, Pontiac convinced many tribes to stop fighting each other and attack English forts. The united Indians quickly captured several English outposts, but the log fort at Detroit held through a summer of war. When leaves began to change color, Indians stopped fighting and returned to their villages to harvest their crops.

Slowly the English won back their forts and again controlled the Great Lakes. To keep the peace, the English set aside land from New York to the western Great Lakes as Indian country. They forbid English settlers from moving into the new territory. But by now the English had also lost control of events in North America.

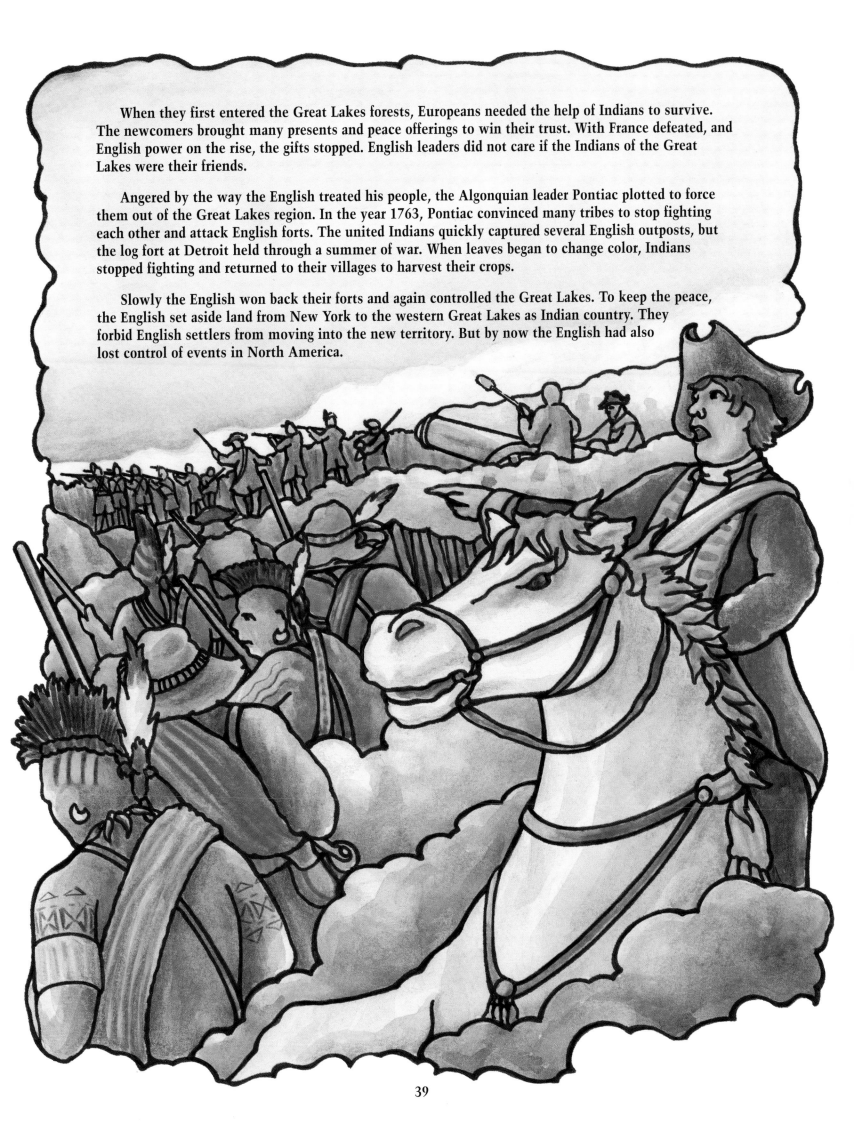

For generations, English colonists lived in close contact with their Iroquois allies. They admired the Iroquois practice of electing their own leaders and Indian laws guaranteeing rights and freedom to every individual. In time, the colonists began to think of themselves as Americans, and did not like being ruled by England.

Many American colonists were angered when the English king demanded high taxes to pay for the war against the French and Indians. In the year 1776, American leaders signed the Declaration of Independence, and the Revolutionary War began. Almost all Indians of the Great Lakes fought with the British against the rebel colonists. The Indians believed that if the colonists won, they would soon invade all Indian lands. The colonists attacked the Iroquois, burning their villages and destroying great fields of corn. The homeland of the most powerful Great Lakes Indian nation lay in ruins.

When the rebel colonists won, a new country, the United States of America, was born. Indian ideas influenced the new country's Constitution, for free people choosing their own leaders was a way of life for the Indians. Writers of the Constitution had studied and published the principles of Iroquois government. Laws uniting the tribes of the Iroquois, whose two-hundred-year-old nation was crushed in the Revolution, lived on in the new United States Constitution.

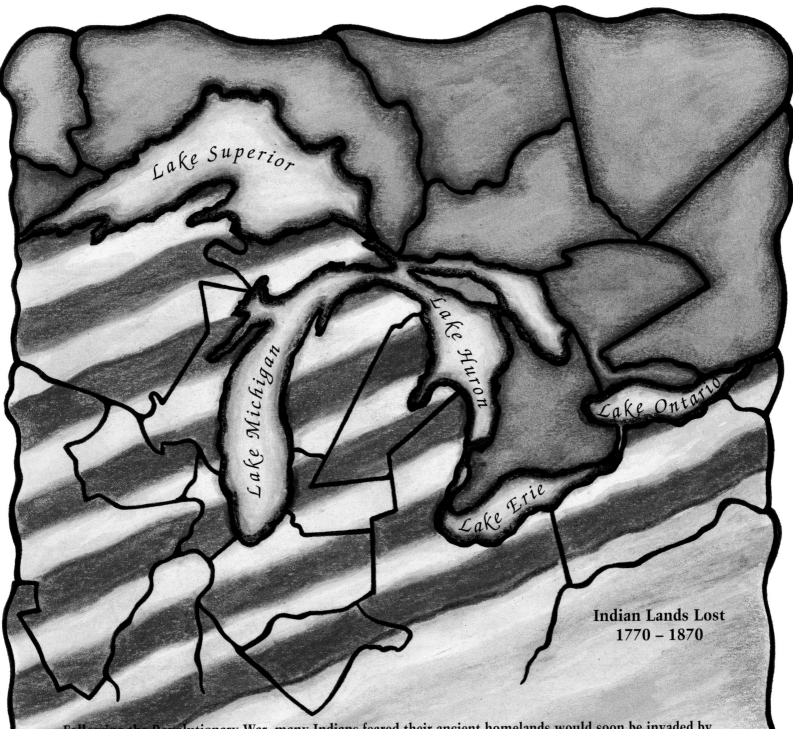

Indian Lands Lost
1770 – 1870

Following the Revolutionary War, many Indians feared their ancient homelands would soon be invaded by settlers from the east. An Indian named Tecumseh traveled the Great Lakes, arguing that all natives were doomed if they did not stand together. All along the Great Lakes, homeless survivors of eastern tribes told sad stories of how they had lost their land. Many Indians rallied around Tecumseh, for the homeless people were living proof his message was true.

In the year 1790, Tecumseh led an Indian army to several victories against United States troops. The Indians of the Great Lakes believed they could finally live in peace. But war and disease had reduced the Great Lakes nations to a fraction of their former size. Many tribes could not forgive their ancient enemies and continued to fight among themselves. Soldiers kept on coming, and piece by piece, defeated Indian leaders signed treaties giving up their lands.

In the year 1832, the Sauk chief, Black Hawk, led his people in a desperate fight to defend their homeland. But by then, few furs were trapped in the Great Lakes country, and fewer Indians lived the ways of their ancestors. There were not many Indians left to fight, and Black Hawk's war ended in disaster. Thirty years later, the Sioux were defeated in the last attempt by Indians of the Great Lakes to hold on to their ancient territory. Only three hundred years after meeting the first Europeans, Native Americans had lost their Great Lakes homeland.

People from all over the world rushed to America for the chance to start a new life. They left countries where they could never afford to own land and came to America, where good land was cheap. Many settlers did not care that the land they wanted belonged to the Indians. They saw the beautiful forests of the Great Lakes as a garden ready to be harvested. Agreements made in treaties with Indian nations were soon forgotten as pioneers poured into the region.

Around the world, many countries entered the Industrial Revolution. Steam-powered metal machines were designed to do the work of dozens of people. The inventions of the Industrial Revolution were soon turned upon the Great Lakes region. Every year, steam-powered saws chewed thousands of acres of forests into boards to build homes. Steamboats carried settlers to the far ends of the Lakes and brought back copper and iron to feed new factories. Railroads and telegraphs linked farms, towns, and cities. The pace of life quickened.

Great Lakes Indians stood by powerless and watched the forests they loved disappear.

During the 1800's, Indians of the Great Lakes were forced to relocate west of the Mississippi River. They settled in Indian Territory, land now known as the state of Oklahoma.

Most Great Lakes natives were forced to abandon the land of their ancestors and move west of the Mississippi River. The new Indian Territory was often very different from the beautiful Great Lakes region. Water was scarce, and poor soil grew few crops. Indians who stayed in the Great Lakes region settled on small pieces of treaty land called reservations.

By the year 1870, the United States was known as the melting pot of the world. People from all nations came to North America and made it their home. Laws governing the United States and Canada made people from the many different countries live by the same new rules. Newcomers gave up the language and ways of their ancestors and worked hard to become Americans.

States carved from the Great Lakes region took their names from Indian words. Lakes and rivers were named to honor Indian leaders. But the Indians of the Great Lakes continued to suffer when new laws changed their ancient traditions. Most early treaties recognized Great Lakes Indians as independent nations within the United States and Canada. But after the military power of the Indians was broken, their freedom as nations ended. Pieces of reservation land were taken from Indian nations. The remaining land was divided among individual Indians and the tribal custom of sharing the land was destroyed.

By the year 1900, the forests surrounding the five Great Lakes had been cut down and the land divided between the United States and Canada. Laws encouraged all people to join in a new American identity. Indian children were taken from their parents and sent to government schools. Their hair was cut, their tribal language forbidden. They were taught to leave the ways of their ancestors behind and join the modern world. Despite the pressure to change, many Indians held on to their identity and taught their children in private the ways of old.

For one hundred years, reservations were places where people of the defeated Indian nations lived with little hope for the future. Indian treaty rights to hunt and fish were restricted, then forgotten. Native people could no longer gather the food they needed from the lakes and woods around them. There were few jobs on reservations, and drinking and despair ruined lives. Reservation populations hit all time lows when Indians left the land of their ancestors for better opportunities. Most who stayed behind began to depend on the government for food and shelter.

Many Native Americans who left the reservation became successful in the modern world. Doctors, scientists, and scholars could trace their ancestors back to Great Lakes Indian nations. Indian steelworkers showed skill and bravery working at heights and built many of North America's tallest buildings. Native American soldiers fought hard and won honors for countries that only one hundred years before had conquered their homelands. Indian writers and poets brought to life stories of their people.

Throughout the land, Indian children sat beside the children of other races and learned to read and write in English. As they grew older, they studied their own history. They saw how treaty rights won in trade for ancestral lands, and their proud and independent way of life, had been lost. They searched for ways their people could regain their rights as Indian nations. Indians looked back to the reservation, the land guaranteed to them by treaty laws. Success in the modern world gave Native Americans the time and money they needed to fight for what was lost.

In recent times, Indians of the Great Lakes have worked hard to build their reservations into centers of power for their people. Now reservations have become the land base where Indian nations again enact and enforce their own laws. Jobs in mining, logging, fishing, gaming and other businesses bring a steady stream of Native Americans back to the reservations. True to ancient traditions, the profits from many reservation businesses are shared by all members of the tribe. Indian population and wealth have climbed. Many Indians of the Great Lakes now live with pride on their reservations and look at them as the best place to determine their own economic and social destiny.

Every year, gatherings called powwows bring Indians of the Great Lakes together on reservations to celebrate their past, present, and future. Traditional dance, dress, and language come alive at the festivals. The ancient rhythm of drums recalls the past greatness of the Indian people and stirs dreams of what will be. The spirit of togetherness that has always been at the heart of Indian traditions is rekindled at the powwows.

As the twenty-first century approaches, Indians of the Great Lakes are regaining the power to determine their own future. As they work to create an Indian vision of tomorrow, they seek to balance their success in the modern world with the traditions of their ancient cultures. For despite the tragedies of the past four hundred years, the native people of the Great Lakes have held onto their Indian identity and now survive with many of their customs and beliefs intact.

Today, all people of the Great Lakes face a complex world filled with many challenges. The ancient forests are gone, but the Great Lakes region remains a rich and important part of the world. For thousands of years, earlier Indians of the Great Lakes lived in harmony with nature by showing respect for all living things. Guided by the spirit of their ancestors, the path modern Indians now choose for their children may lead us all into a better future.